BOULEVARD BOOKS
The New Face of Publishing
www.BoulevardBooks.org

ISBN 13: 978-1-942500-64-3

THE **BIG** PRESCHOOL & KINDERGARDEN MATH WORKBOOK

FOR

TODDLERS

AGED 2-4

Count and Match.

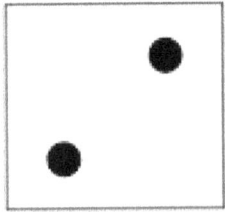

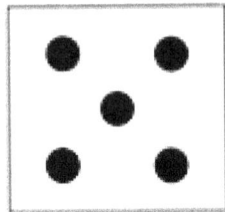

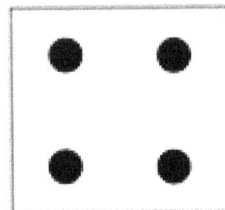

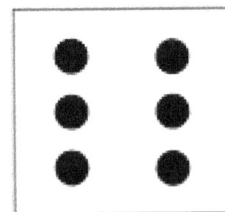

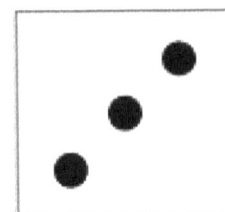

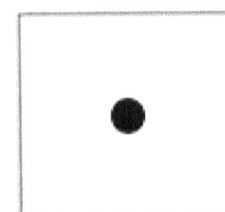

5

4

2

3

6

1

Mittens counting sheet

How many mittens can you see in each row? Color and count the mittens and circle the correct number below in each row.

1   4   5   2   3

7   0   3   9   6

5   4   8   1   3

1   6   9   10   4

Addition with dots

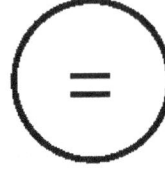

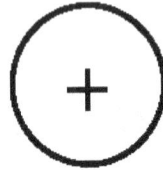

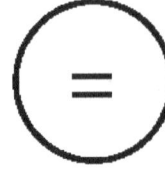

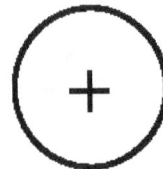

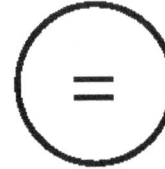

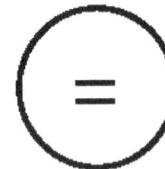

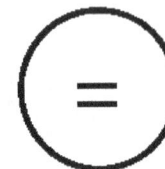

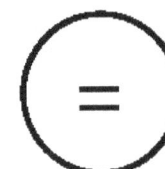

2 ••	+	2 ••	=	
5 •••••	+	4 ••••	=	
4 ••••	+	3 •••	=	
3 •••	+	3 •••	=	
4 ••••	+	4 ••••	=	
5 •••••	+	3 •••	=	

I Spy

MATH FUN

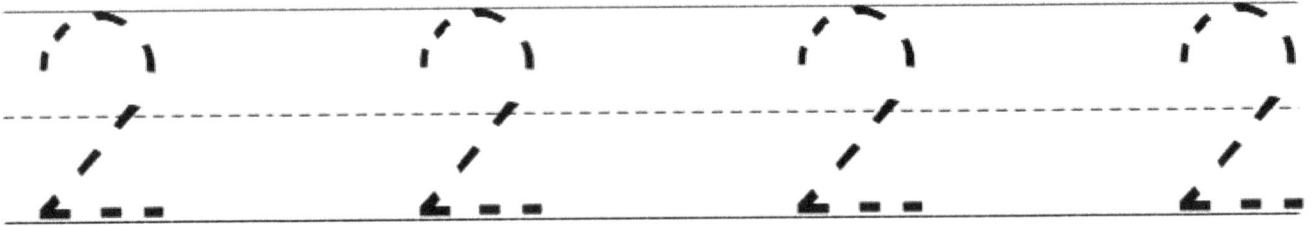

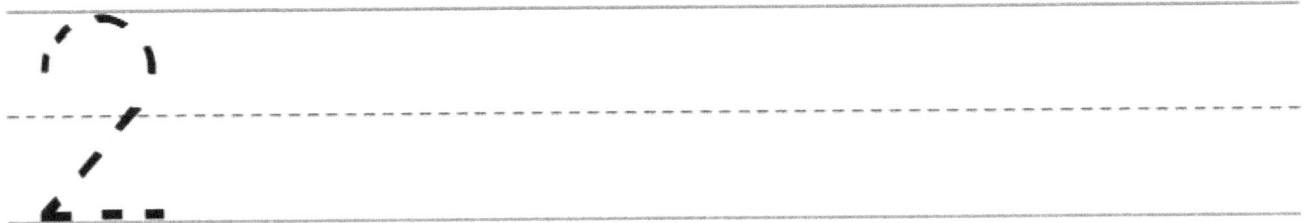

Circle 2 cowboys

Color 2 boots

Preschool Math Worksheet

Redraw the following figures and name them.

SQUARE	
CIRCLE	
RECTANGLE	
TRIANGLE 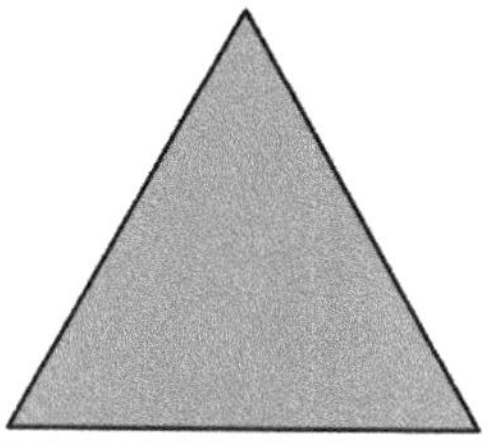	
OVAL	

You are SMART!

You are SMART!

Name_____

Numbers 1 - 5

one   2

two   4

three   1

four   5

five   3

8

LET'S PRACTICE OUR NUMBERS

1		3		5			8		10
11				15		17		19	
21		23			26			29	
31		33		35			38		40
	42		44			47		49	

NUMBERS

1-Brown 2-Red 3-Green 4-Yellow

Find the matching mitten pairs and color them in.

11

My Five Senses

Name _____

Draw lines between the pictures and the words that best go together.

Taste

Touch

See

Smell

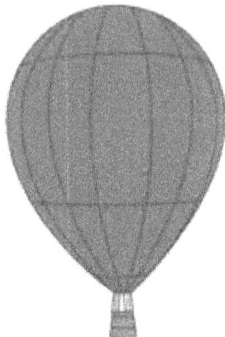

Hear

Count the items on each row and circle the corresponding number.

1 3 2

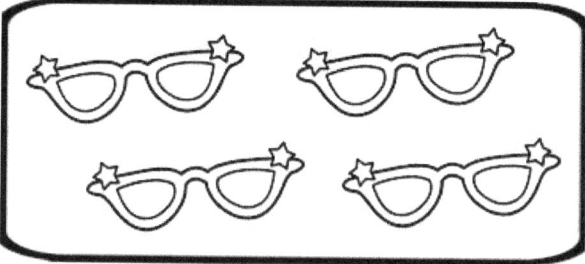

5 4 2

4 2 1

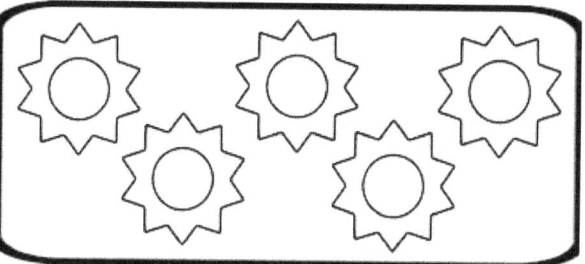

3 5 4

2 1 3

Mittens counting sheet

How many mittens can you see in each row? Color and count the mittens and circle the correct number below in each row.

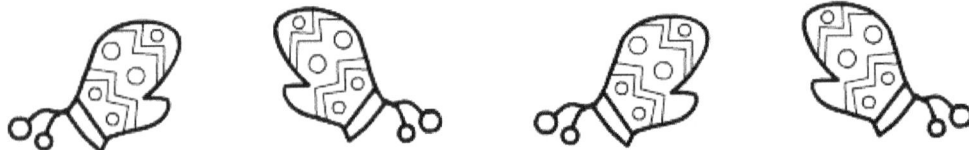

1   4   5   2   3

7   0   3   9   6

5   4   8   1   3

1   6   9   10   4

Circle all the 11s in the number scramble below

$$\bigcirc 11$$

11	16	12	11	15
10	13	14	11	18
11	19	11	14	15
17	12	13	11	10
14	11	18	17	16

Spell It Out

Add. Complete the puzzle using number words.

Across

1. 5 + 5 = _____

2. 3 + _____ = 7

3. 2 + _____ = 9

6. 6 + 2 = _____

7. _____ + 0 = 1

Down

1. 4 + _____ = 6

2. 2 + _____ = 7

3. _____ + 4 = 10

4. 4 + 5 = _____

5. 5 + _____ = 8

Finish each number sentence with a number word.

five + two = _____   three + six = _____

A Great Catch

Circle each group of 10. Write the number of tens and ones on the chart. Then write the number on the baseball glove.

tens	ones
1	3

tens	ones

tens	ones

tens	ones

tens	ones

tens	ones

tens	ones

tens	ones

DICE THROW MITTEN

Directions:
Take two dice and toss them. Add the dice together and then color that number!

5
11
9
7
10
4
8
2
6
3
12

Recognizing Shapes

Name:_____

Color each shape

Square

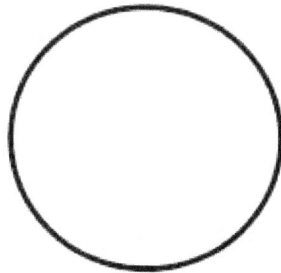

Circle

Rectangle

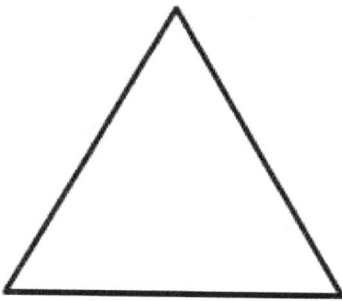

Triangle

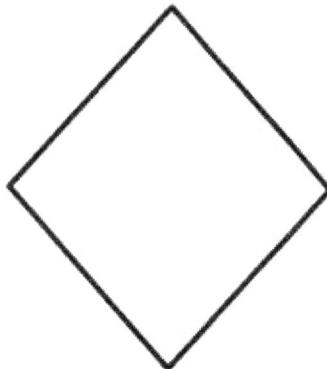

Diamond

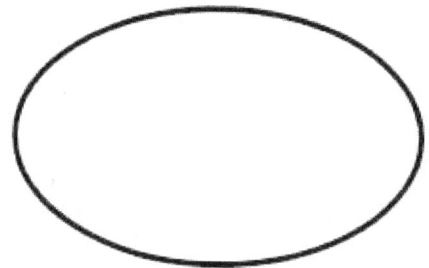

Oval

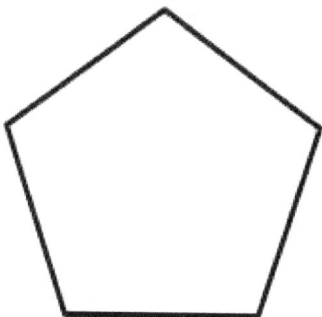

Pentagon

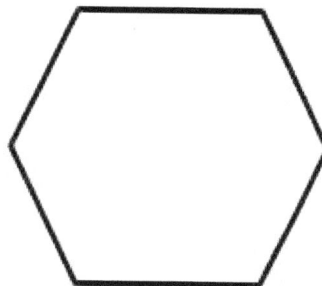

Hexagon

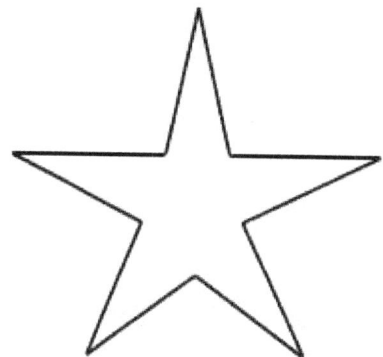

Star

Recognizing Shapes

Name:_____

Connect shapes with a line

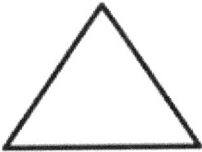

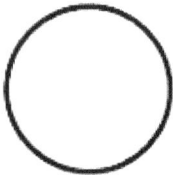

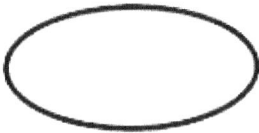

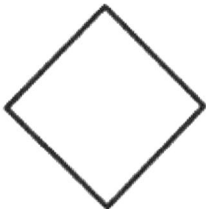

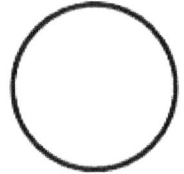

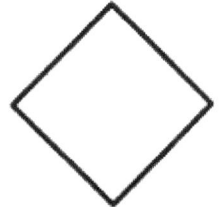

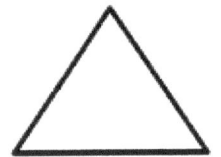

Color all the rectangle shapes orange.

Color all the oval shapes green.

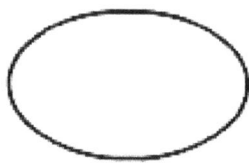

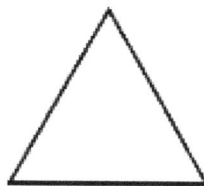

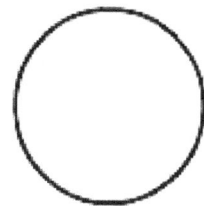

Color all the heart shapes red.

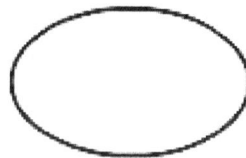

Color all the circle shapes pink.

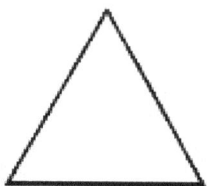

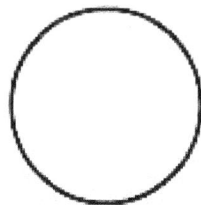

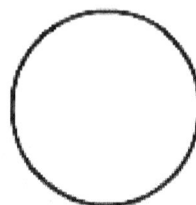

Color all the triangle shapes blue.

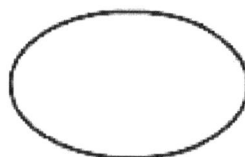

Name : _____

Number Practice

Trace it.

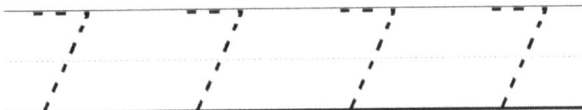

Write it.

_____

Tally it.

Trace it.

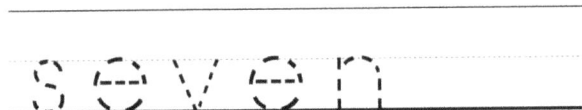

Write it.

_____

Draw it.

Circle all the number 7.

Color seven.

COLORING FUN

RIDE THE NUMBERS
CHOO-CHOO TRAIN

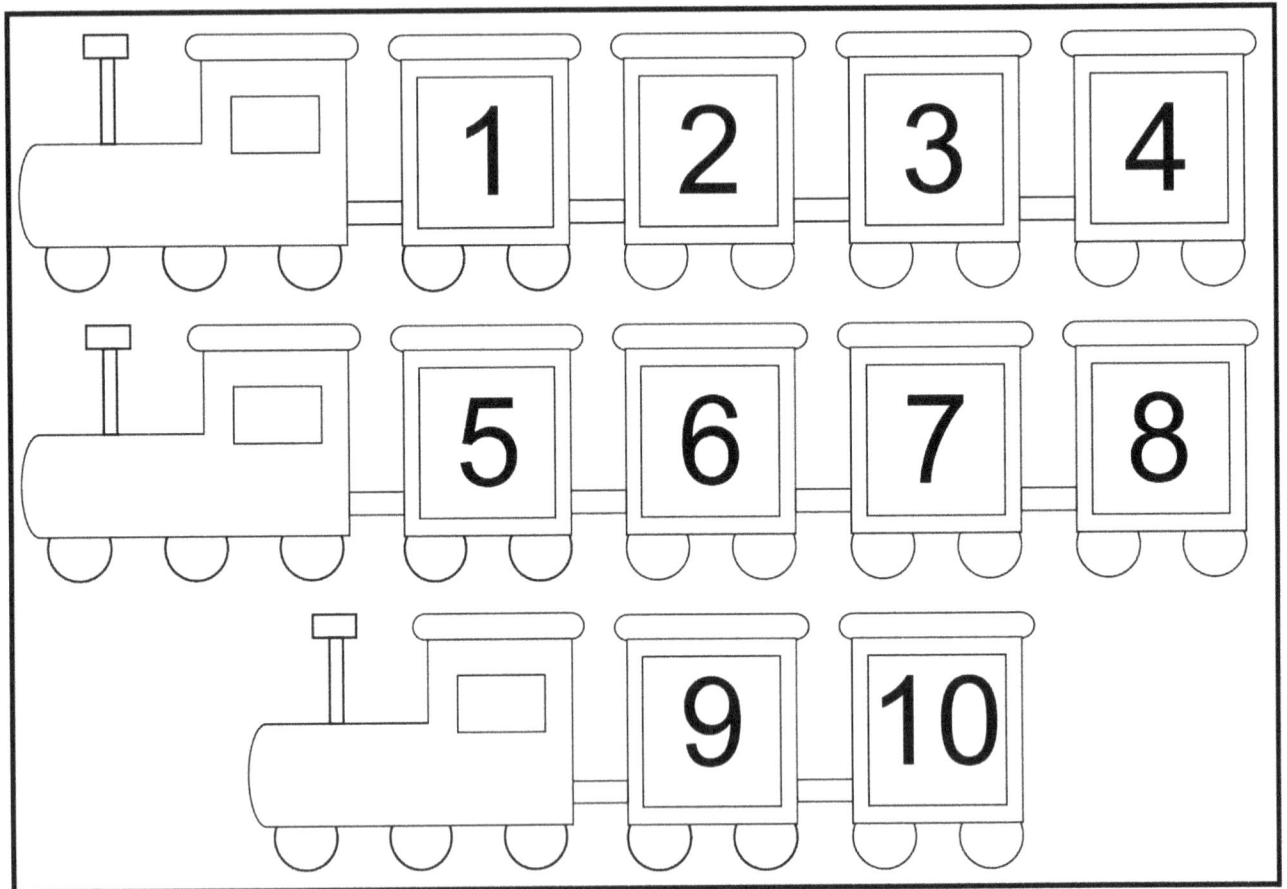

1 2 3 4

5 6 7 8

9 10

Spring Bonds

Directions: Find the missing numbers. Color the pictures.

7 / 3 __	3 / 1 __	10 / 6 __
5 / 2 __	9 / 4 __	2 / 1 __
4 / 1 __	6 / 4 __	8 / 7 __

TRACING AND WRITING NUMBERS 1-5

	1	1	1	1	1
	2	2	2	2	2
	3	3	3	3	3
	4	4	4	4	4
	5	5	5	5	5

🦩	+	[ ]
🌿 🌿	+ 🦩	[ ]
🦩	+ 🦩	[ ]
💐 💐	+ 🌹🌹	[ ]
🌿 🌿	+ 🦩🦩🦩	[ ]

1	**2**	**3**	**4**	**5**

HOW MANY DOGGIES ARE THERE?

2 + 1 = ___

1 + 3 = ___

1 + 2 = ___

3 + 2 = ___

ACORN MATH

Squirrel has buried ten acorns. Circle the even numbers. Put an "X" on the odd numbers. Color the picture.

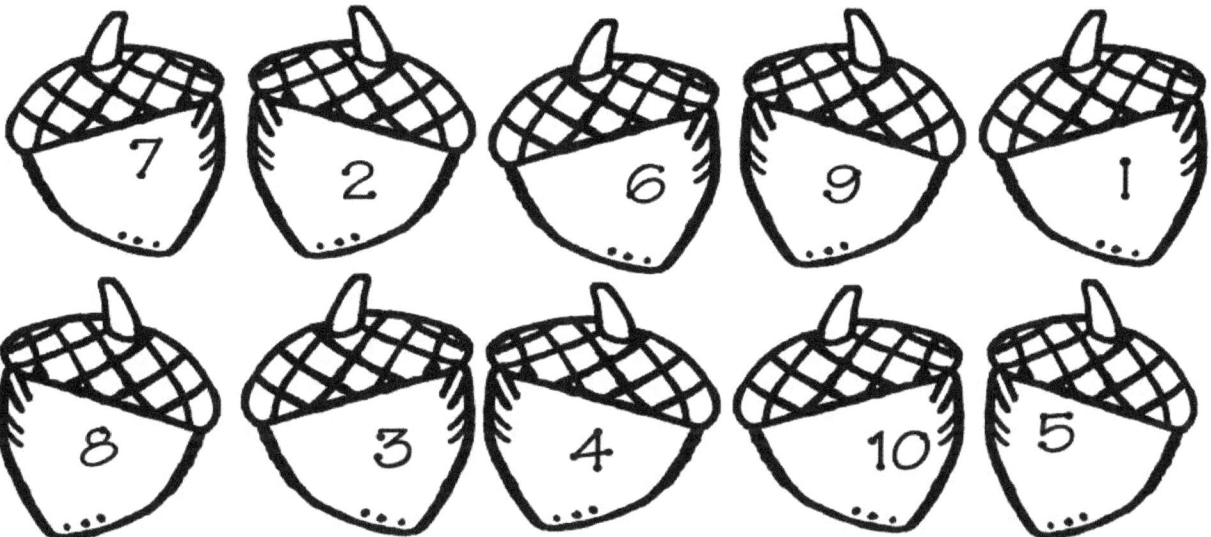

7 2 6 9 1

8 3 4 10 5

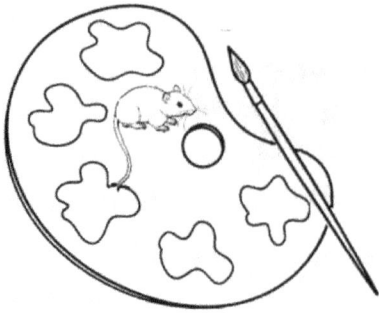

The mice had fun blending the colors to make new colors. Now you can too! Paint the two color circles, and then combine to make a new color.

Red + Yellow = Orange

 +  =

Blue + Yellow = Green

 +  =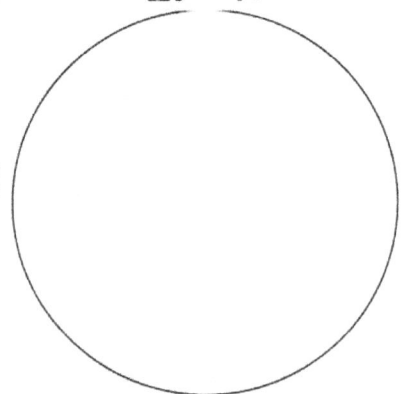

Blue + Red = Purple

 +  =

Telling Time

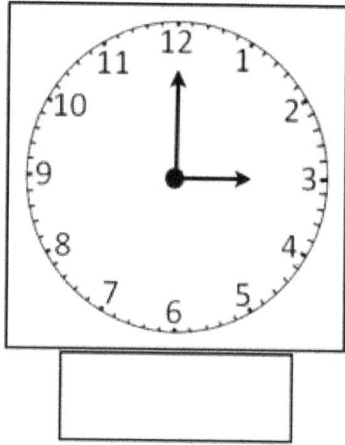

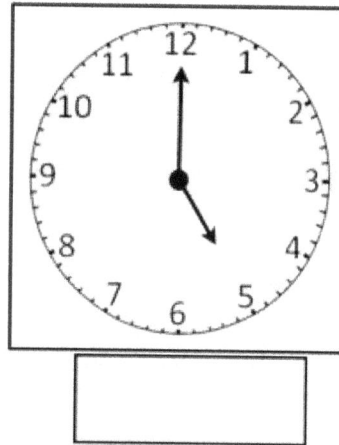

2:00

3:00

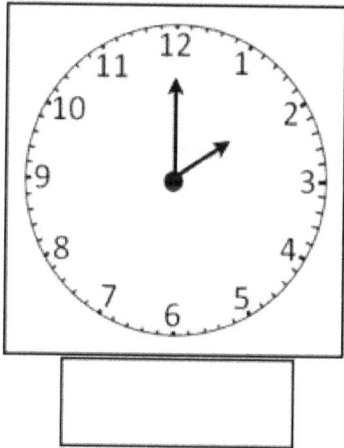

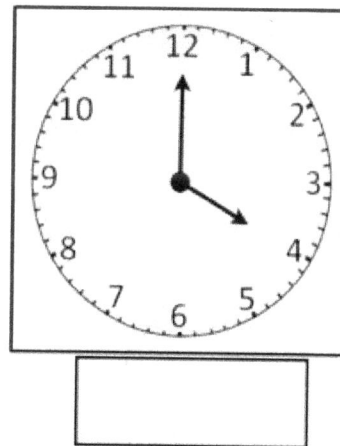

4:00

5:00

31

Spring Skip Counting by 5's

Directions: Skip count by 5's and write the missing numbers on each umbrella.

5   15

30   40

55   65

80   90

105   115

ORNAMENT ⭐ NOTES

Color the A pink
Color the B green.
Color the C orange
Color the D yellow

Color the E purple.
Color the F's blue.
Color the G's red.
Color the Christmas tree.

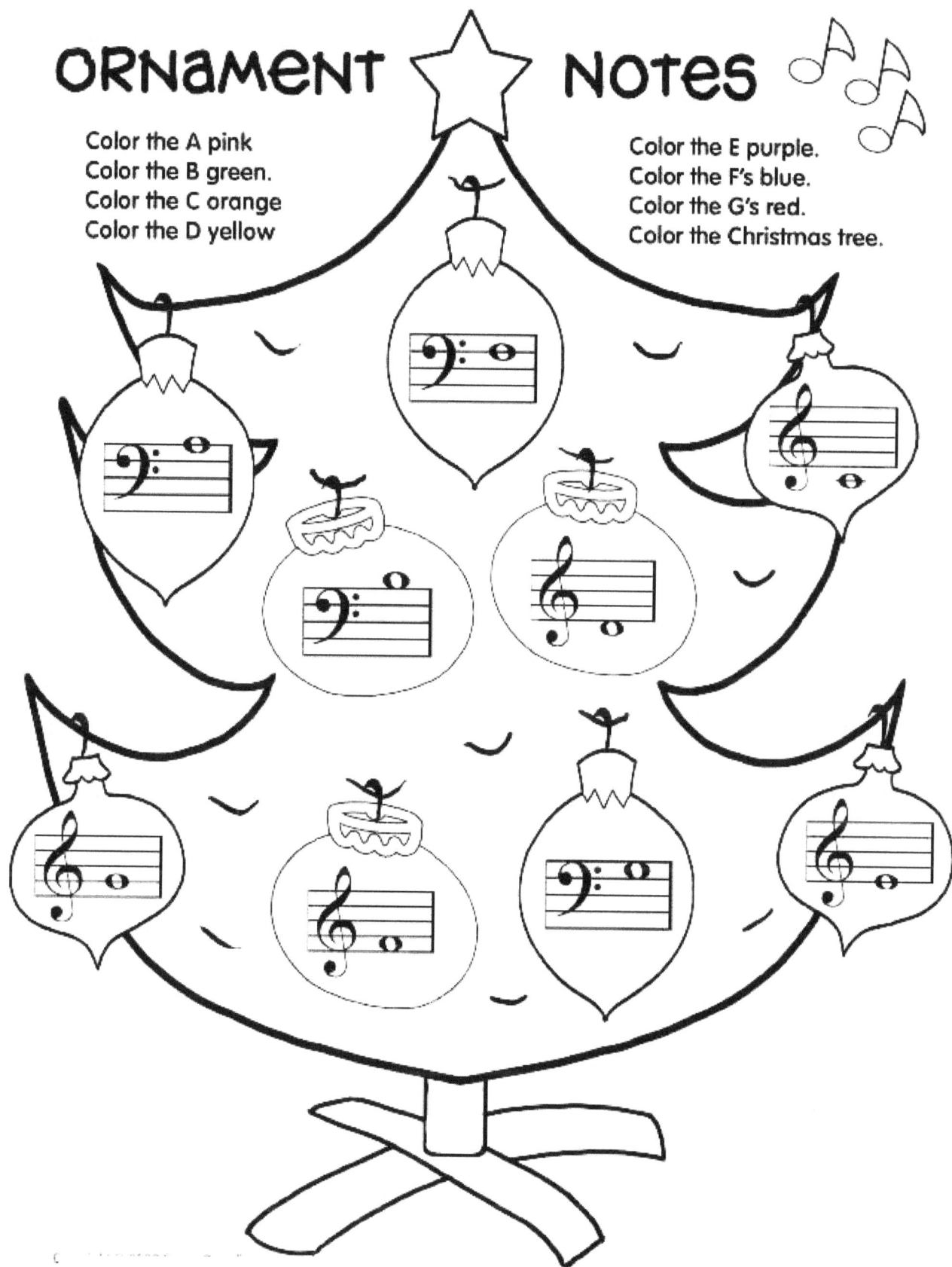

33

Tucker Turtle

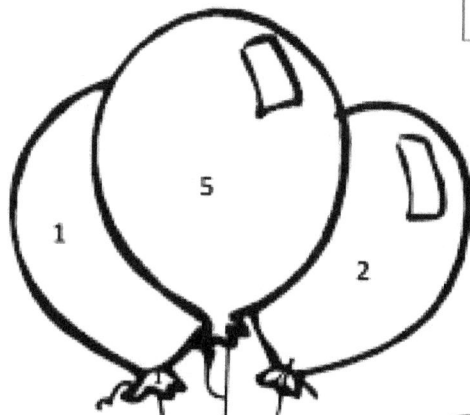

Red 1
Yellow 2
Green 3
Purple 4
Blue 5
Brown 6

1+1= ☐

1+3= ☐

1+2= ☐

1+7= ☐

1+4= ☐

1+8= ☐

1+9= ☐

1+10= ☐

1+5= ☐

1+6= ☐

Count and circle the correct answer

	3 4 1 2
	5 4 3 2
	4 6 3 5
	4 3 1 2
	2 4 5 3

Find it

Circle the picture in each row that does not belong the group.

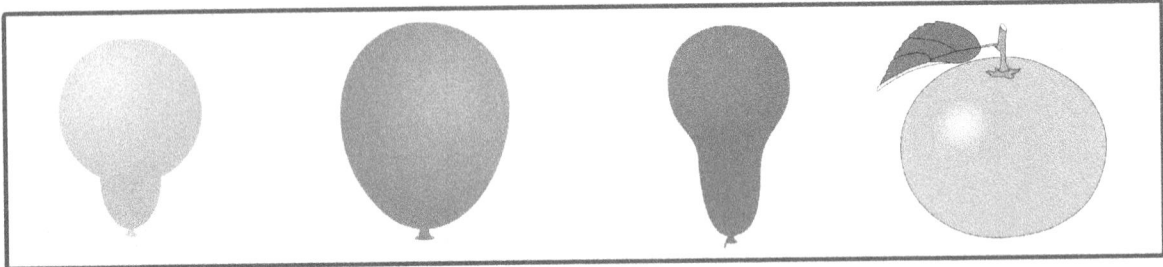

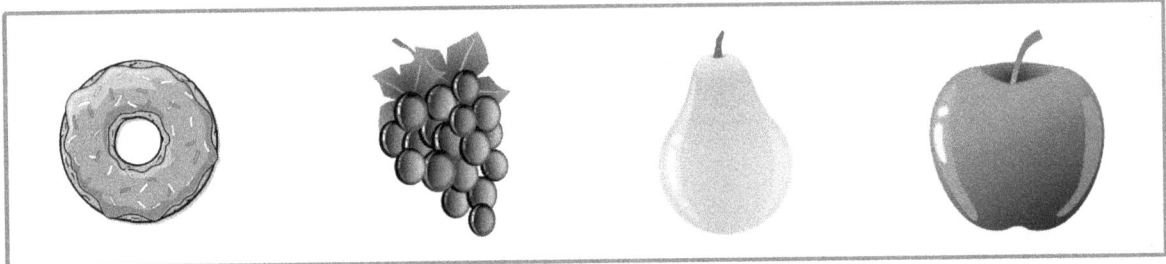

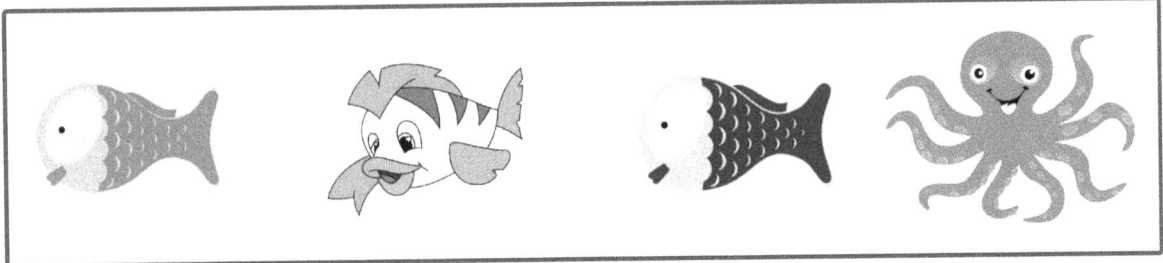

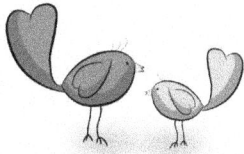

Match it

Draw a line from each baby to its parent. Name the animal.

Match it

Name each object. Connect the objects that go together.

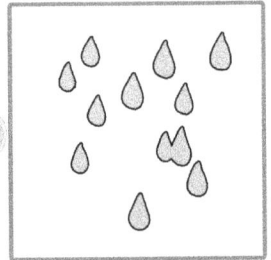

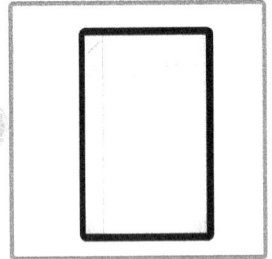

Find it

Circle the 2 picture in each row that go together.

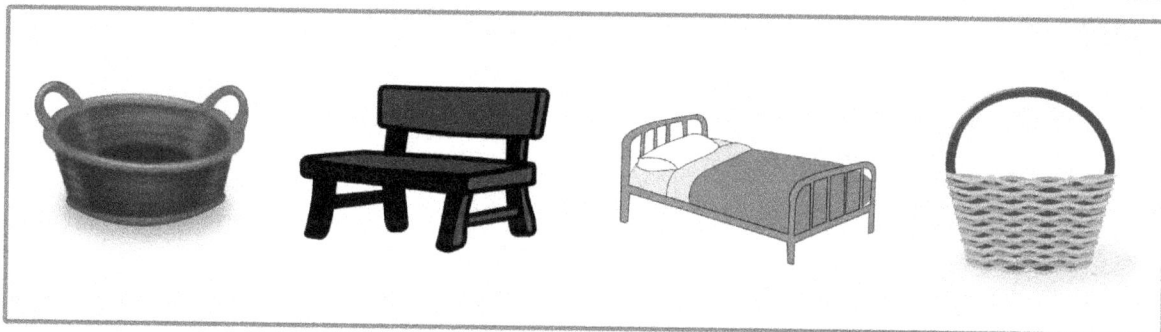

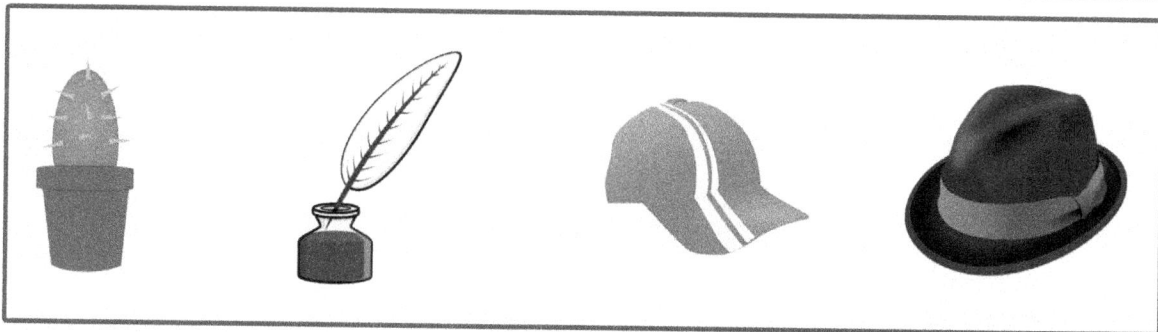

Match it

Name each object. Connect the objects that go together.

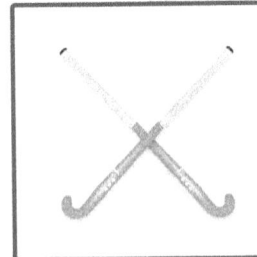

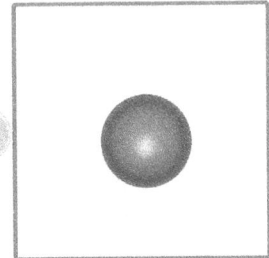

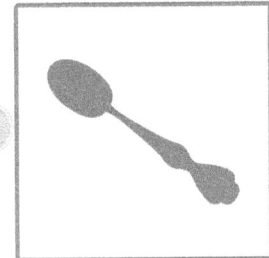

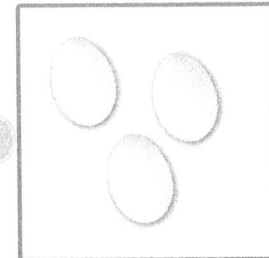

Draw a line from each shape on the left to the matching shape on the right side of the page.

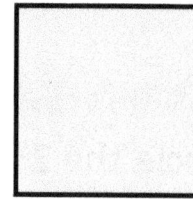

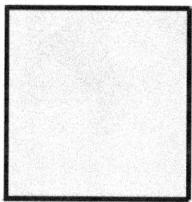

Find it

Circle the 2 picture in each row that go together.

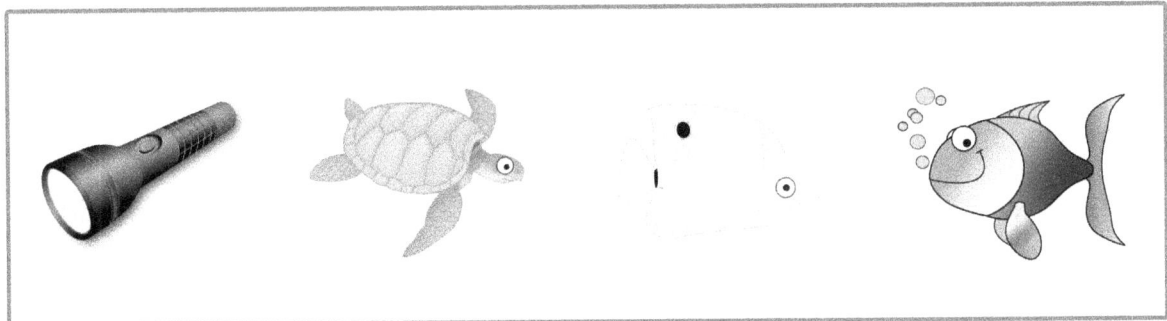

| 3 | 1 | 4 | 2 | 3 | 1 |

| 4 | 2 | 3 | 1 | 4 | 2 |

MATCH IT UP SHEET 6

Draw lines to connect the numbers and shapes that go together.

3   

4   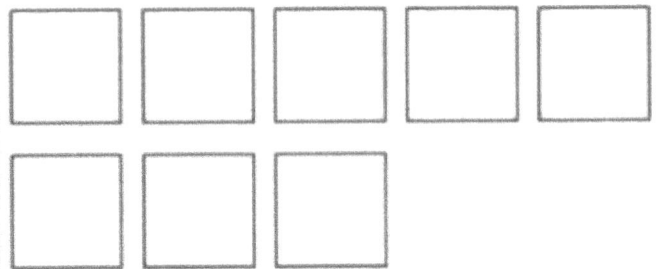

5   

6   

7   

8   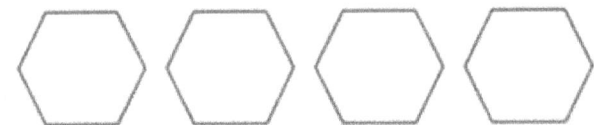

 **+**  **=**

 **+** 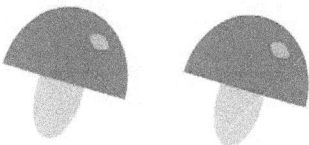 **=**

 **+**  **=**

Find it

Circle the picture in each row that does not belong the group.

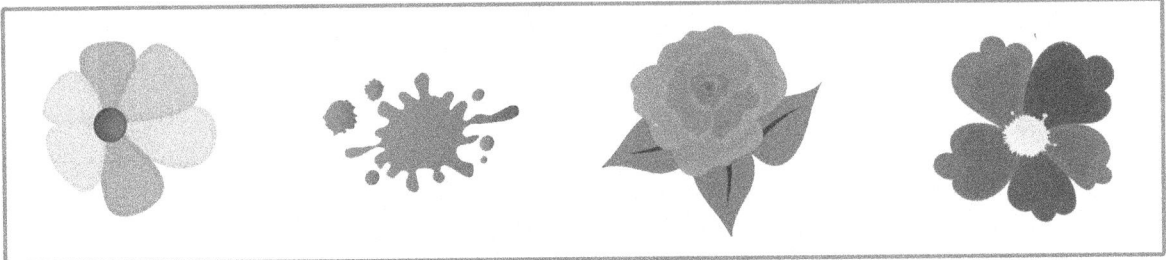

 +  =

 + 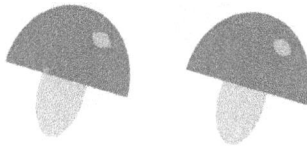 =

 +  =

COLOR THE NUMBERS

1 2 3 4 5 6

7 8 9 10 11 12

13 14 15 16

17 18 19 20

Choose

> = <

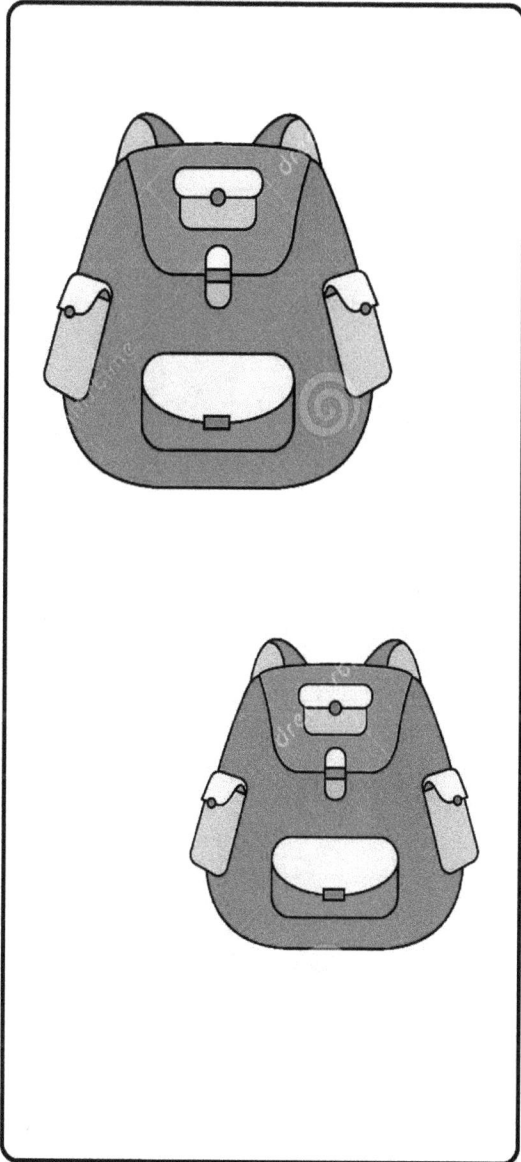  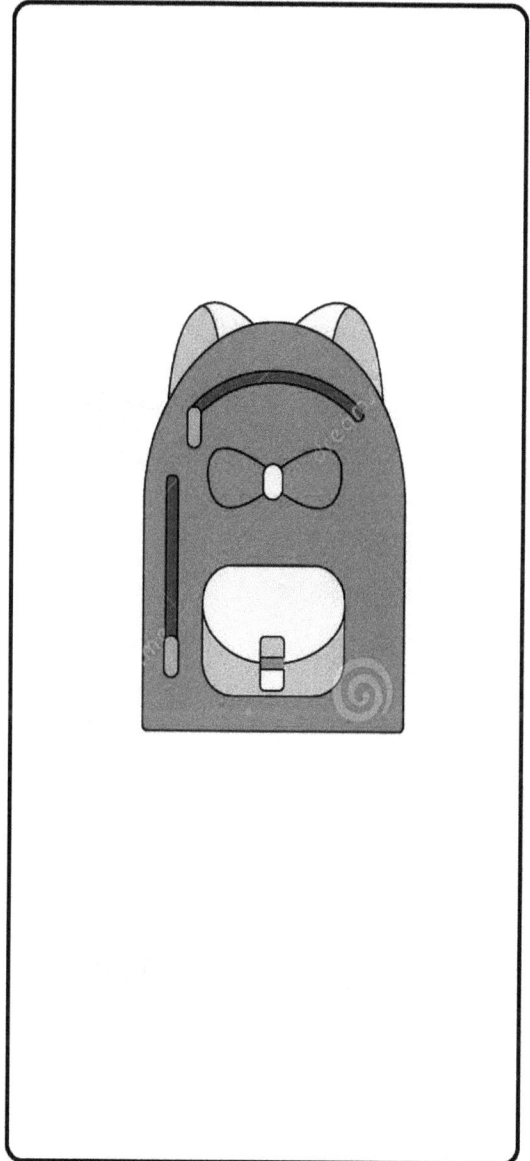

Choose

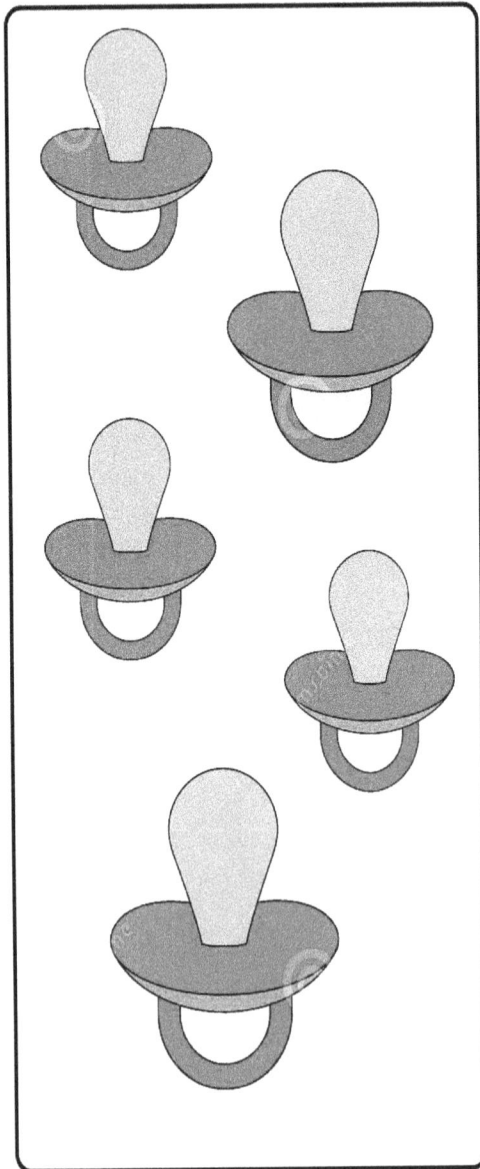

Choose

> = <

Choose

> = <

Find it

Circle the 2 picture in each row that go together.

Find it

Circle the picture in each row that does not belong the group.

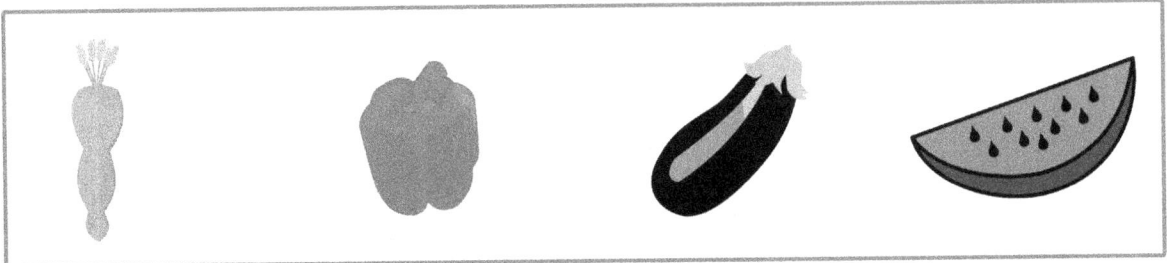

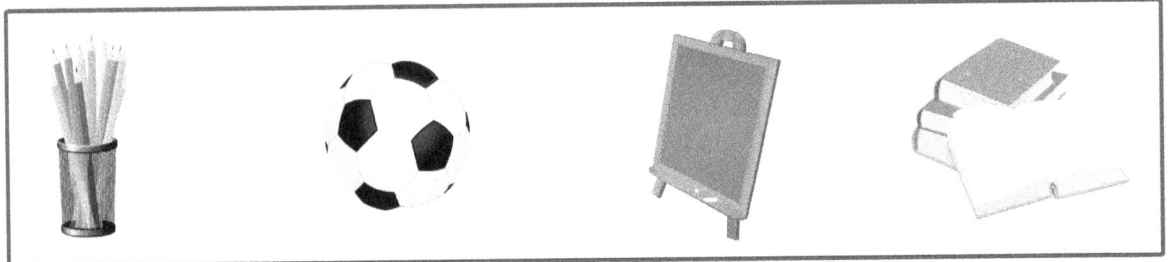

 +  = [ ]

 + 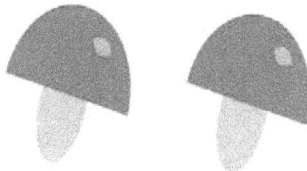 = [ ]

 +  = [ ]

1

2

3

4

5

6

7

8

9

1-10

1	2	3	4	5
			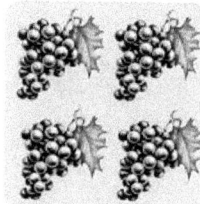	

6	7	8	9	10
		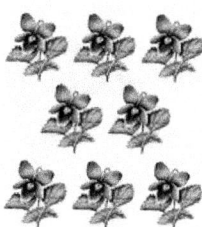		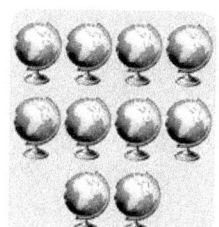

Puzzle +

1+0	1+1	2+1	1+3	2+3
+	+	+	+	+
1	2	3	4	5

2+4	4+3	5+3	4+5	2+8
+	+	+	+	+
6	7	8	9	10

Puzzle -

10-1	10-2	9-2	9-3	7-2
9	8	7	6	5

8-4	7-4	3-1	5-4	1-1
4	3	2	1	0

61

Name : _____

Number Practice

Trace it.

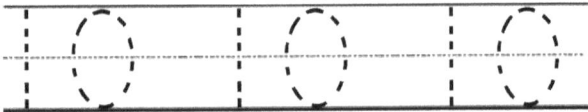

Write it.

_____

Tally it.

Trace it.

Write it.

_____

Draw it.

Circle all the number 10.

2   10   4   5

10   3   10

8

7   10   6

1   9

10   10   10

Color ten.

Practice counting to twenty (20)
by filing in the missing
numbers below.

| 1 | | | 4 | | 6 | | 8 | 9 | |
| 11 | | 13 | | 15 | | 17 | | | 20 |

| | 2 | 3 | | 5 | | | | | 10 |
| | 12 | | | | 16 | | | 19 | |

| 1 | | 3 | | | | 7 | | 9 | |
| | 12 | | 14 | | | | | | 20 |

| | | 3 | | 5 | | | 8 | | 10 |
| 11 | | | | | 16 | 17 | | | |

Practice counting to hundred (100)
by filing in the missing
numbers below.

		3	4						10
					16				
21							28		
			35						
	42					47			
		54						59	
61									
	73			76					
			85						90
	92								

Shamrock Frames

Color the shamrocks to match the number.

11

13

16

19

18

15

STAR Counting 1-20

1	2		4
	6		8
		11	
13			16
17		19	

14	12	3	9	18
20	15	5	10	7

Number Chart 1-10

1	2	3
4	5	6
7	8	9
	10	

Number Recognition Assessment

3	5	2	4
8	10	6	7
9	12	20	15
11	14	16	18
19	17	13	1

STAR Counting 1-20

1	2		4
	6		8
		11	
13			16
17		19	

14	12	3	9	18
20	15	5	10	7

Match the number of stars in the left column to the number in the right column

1.    9

2.    14

3.    17

4.    11

Number COUNT & MATCH

Direction : Count the picture and match the number.

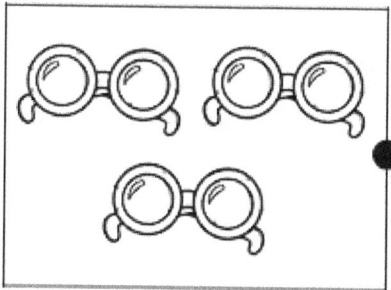

1

2

3

4

5

Count n' Match

Draw a line between each set of dots and the correct number.

10      12

19      16

15      20

11

17      13

18      14

Hopsalot Says: Save 11 juice cans. Cover them with construction paper and label them with the numbers 10 to 20. Gather a supply of dried beans. Ask your child to place the corresponding number of beans in each can. To check your child's work, turn the cans over and count the beans together.

72

COLOR BY NUMBERS

6- Blue
7- Black
8- Purple
9- Yellow

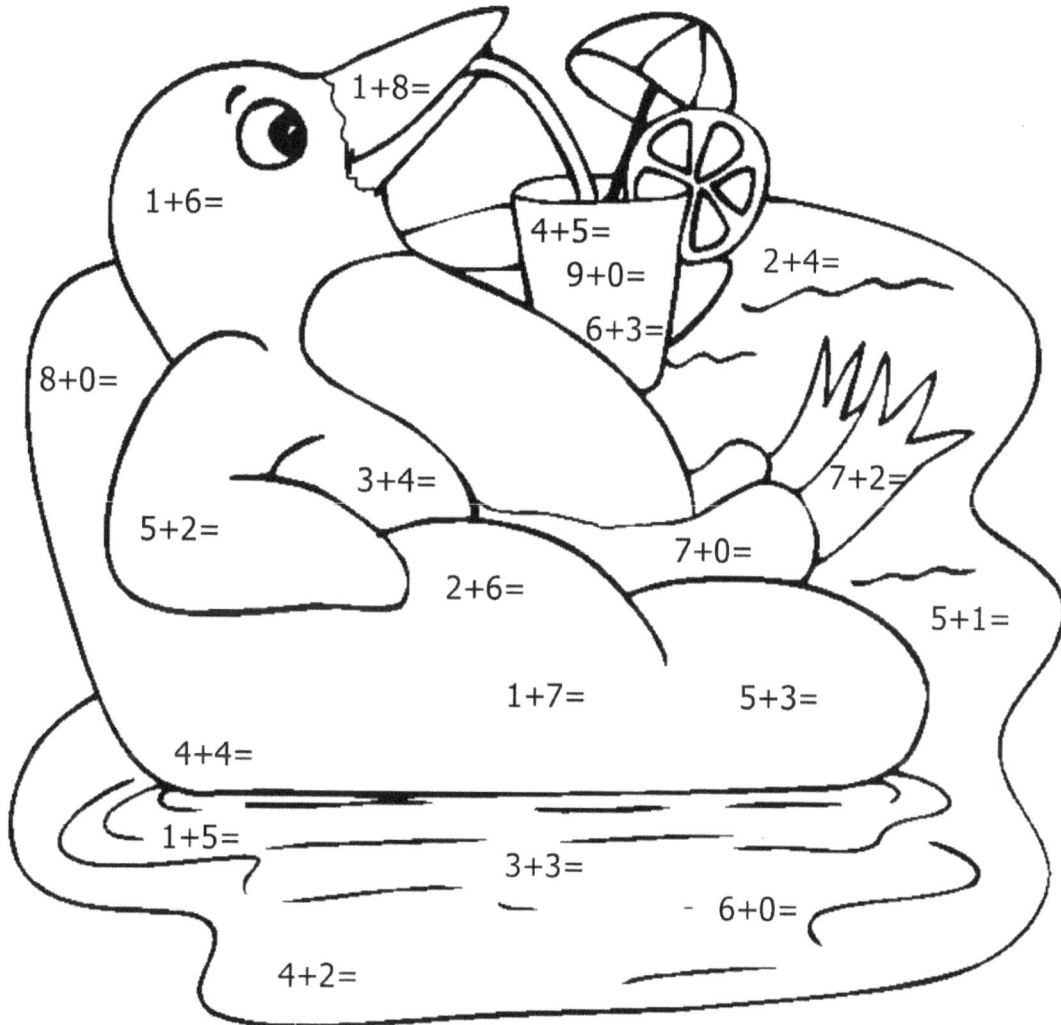

1+8=

1+6=

4+5=

9+0=

6+3=

2+4=

8+0=

3+4=

7+2=

5+2=

7+0=

2+6=

5+1=

1+7=

5+3=

4+4=

1+5=

3+3=

6+0=

4+2=

2-Blue 3-Yellow 4-Red 5-Green

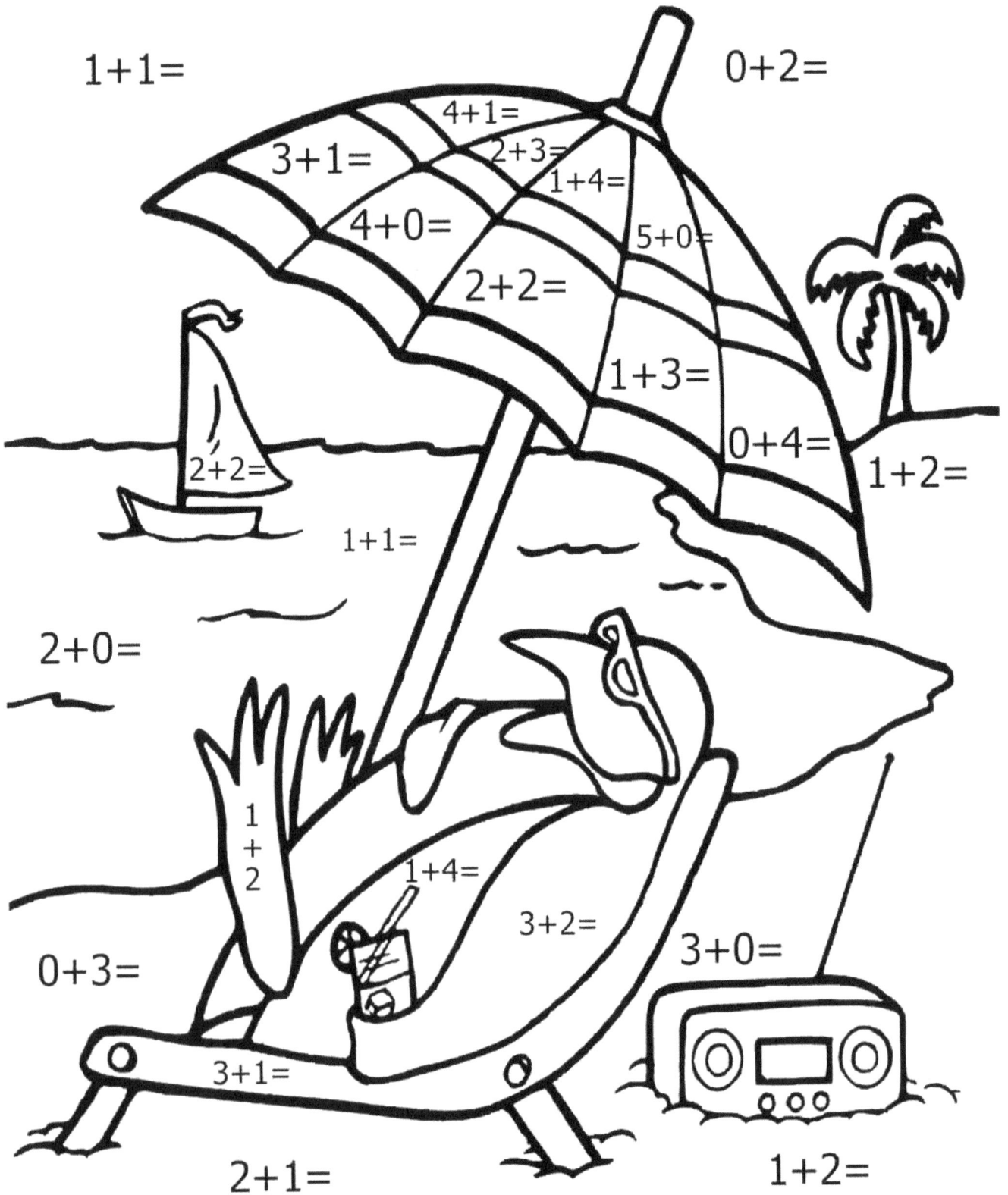

1+1=

0+2=

4+1=

3+1=

2+3=

1+4=

4+0=

5+0=

2+2=

1+3=

0+4=

1+2=

2+2=

1+1=

2+0=

1
+
2

1+4=

3+2=

3+0=

0+3=

3+1=

2+1=

1+2=

Directions: write the answer to each subtraction problem. Color each part of the picture using the color code.

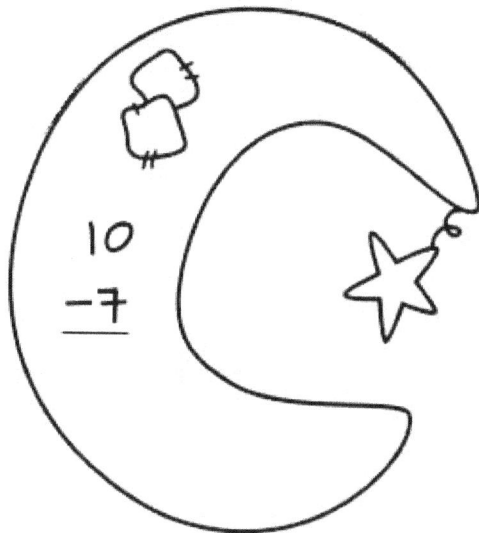

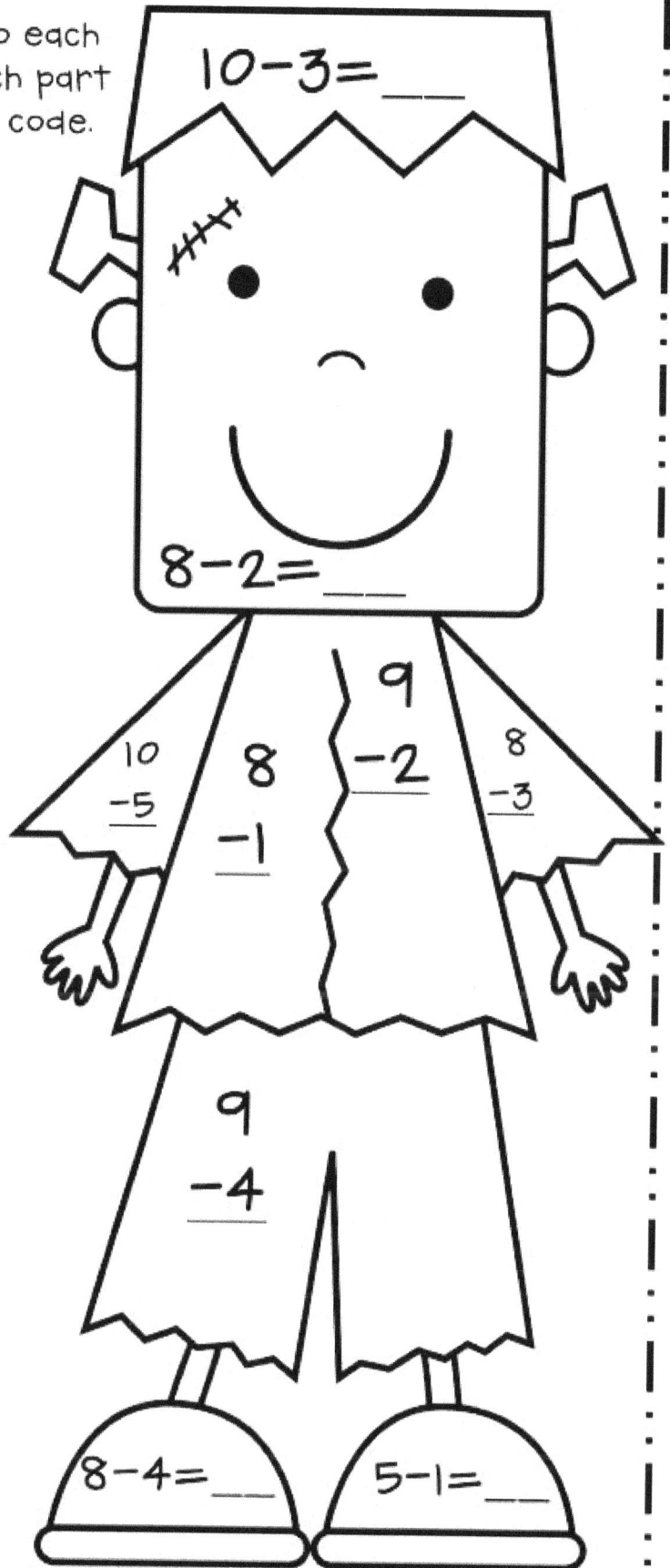

$10-3=$ ___

$\begin{array}{r} 10 \\ -7 \\ \hline \end{array}$

$8-2=$ ___

$\begin{array}{r} 10 \\ -5 \\ \hline \end{array}$

$\begin{array}{r} 8 \\ -1 \\ \hline \end{array}$

$\begin{array}{r} 9 \\ -2 \\ \hline \end{array}$

$\begin{array}{r} 8 \\ -3 \\ \hline \end{array}$

$\begin{array}{r} 9 \\ -4 \\ \hline \end{array}$

$8-4=$ ___

$5-1=$ ___

color code

7-Black

6=Green

5=Purple

4=Red

3=Yellow

3+1 =

3+3 =

6+1 =

COLOR
THE
NUMBERS

Golden **Number Bonds**

9 — ◯ / 3

4 — 0 / ◯

8 — ◯ / 2

7 — 6 / ◯

10 — 7 / ◯

5 — ◯ / 5

Fish Facts

Use the key to color the fish.

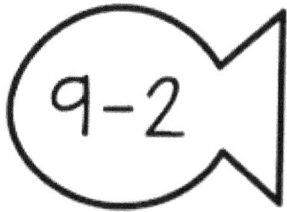

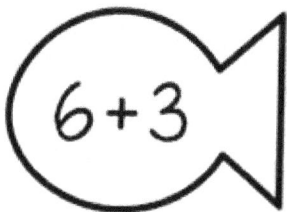

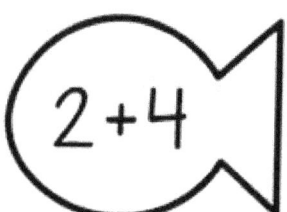

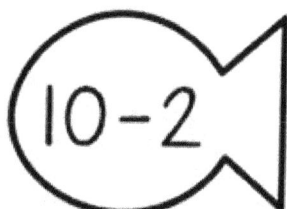

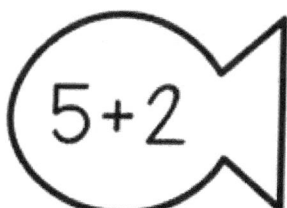

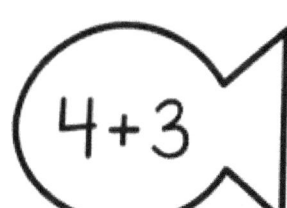

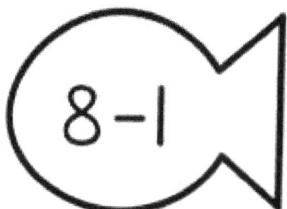

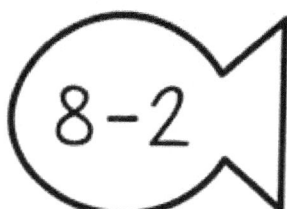

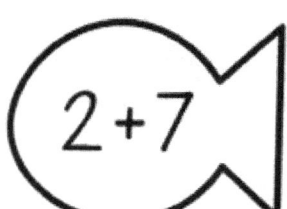

9-2	6+3	2+4	4+4
3+3	10-2	3+5	10-1
5+4	5+2	7-1	4+3
8-1	8-2	2+7	9-1

pink 6   green 8

red 7   yellow 9

Name _____

COUNT How Many 4 5 6

Count how many objects are in each box.
Color the correct number.

5 cats — ④ ⑤ ⑥	2 boots — ④ ⑤ ⑥	6 logs — ④ ⑤ ⑥

5 whales — ④ ⑤ ⑥	4 pretzels — ④ ⑤ ⑥	6 hats — ④ ⑤ ⑥

4 glasses — ④ ⑤ ⑥	5 bows — ④ ⑤ ⑥	6 birds — ④ ⑤ ⑥

Cut out the pumpkins.
Paste them in the correct number order.

10   5   7   2   9

4   1   8   3   6

6 Ways to Make Number 1

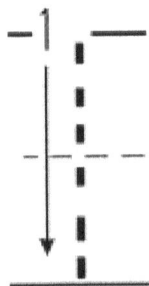

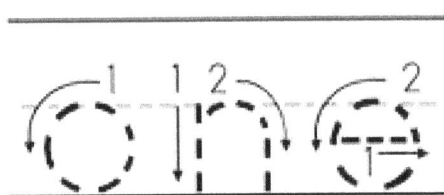

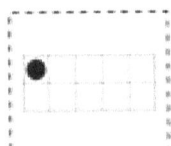

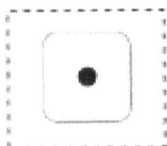

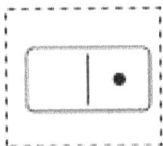

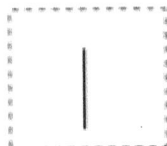

one

Paste

one

Numbers 1-10

Directions: Trace the numbers from 1-10 in each set.
Fill in the missing numbers.

1			4	5
6		8		10

	2	3		5
	7		9	

	2	3	4	
6		8		

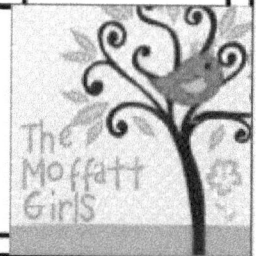

The Moffatt Girls

83

Numbers 1-10

1	2	3	4	5
6	7	8	9	10

Math Quiz

1. Fill in the blanks

$$4 + 3 = \boxed{} \qquad 5 + 2 = \boxed{}$$

2. Color and count the leaves

3. Fill in the missing numbers

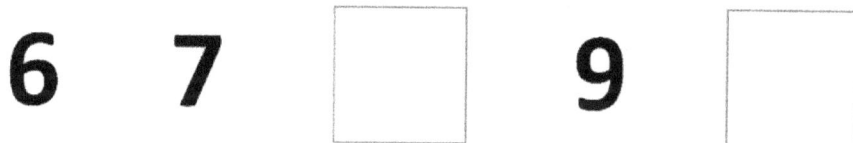

$$6 \quad 7 \quad \boxed{} \quad 9 \quad \boxed{}$$

4. Draw the next shape in the sequence

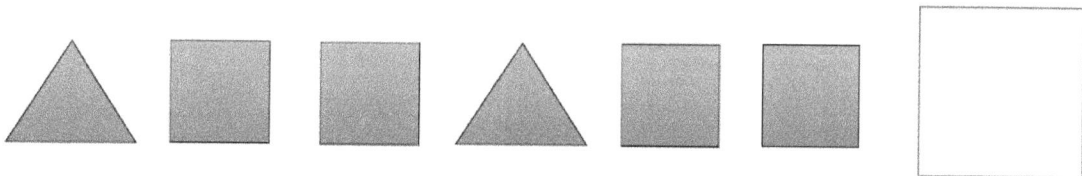

5. Write the number that comes before and after

	3			8	

Name_____

Count the snowflakes. Cut and paste the numbers that match.

1

2

3

4

5

6

Name:——————

Summer
Number counting

(1) (2) (3)

(5) (6) (7)

(3) (4) (5)

(3) (4) (5)

(4) (5) (6)

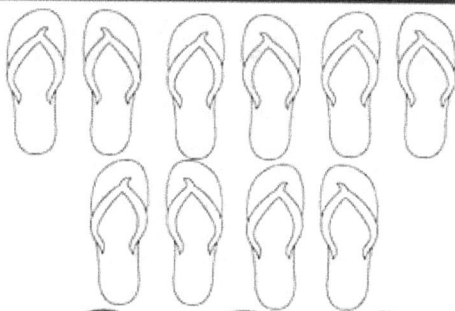

(8) (9) (10)

Directions: How many are there? Count and color.

Name _____

COUNT How Many

Count how many objects are in each box.
Color the correct number.

4 5 6	4 5 6	4 5 6
4 5 6	4 5 6	4 5 6
4 5 6	4 5 6	4 5 6

FLOWER meASUREMENTS

count and color the total number of cubes tall for each flower.

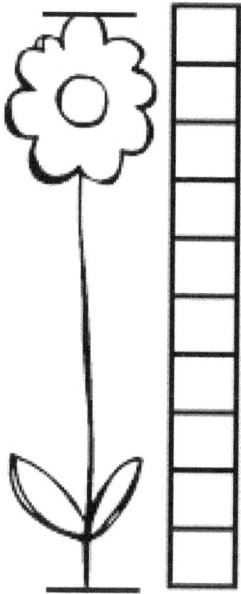

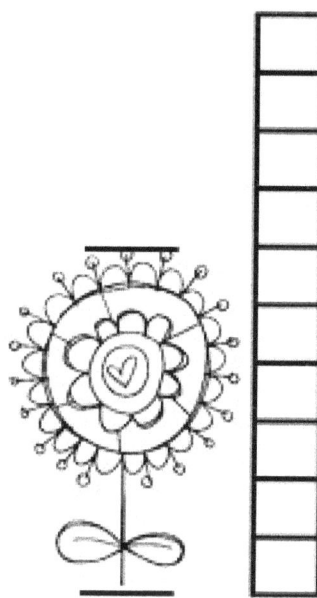

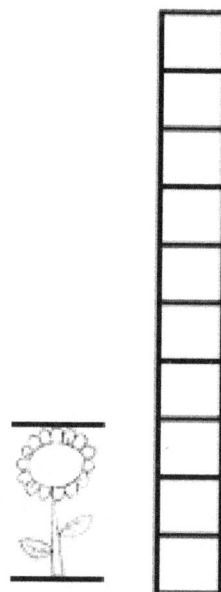

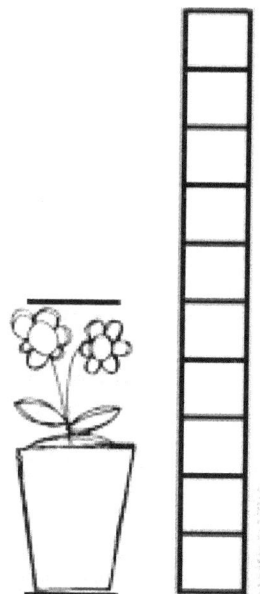

Addition

Add and write the number.

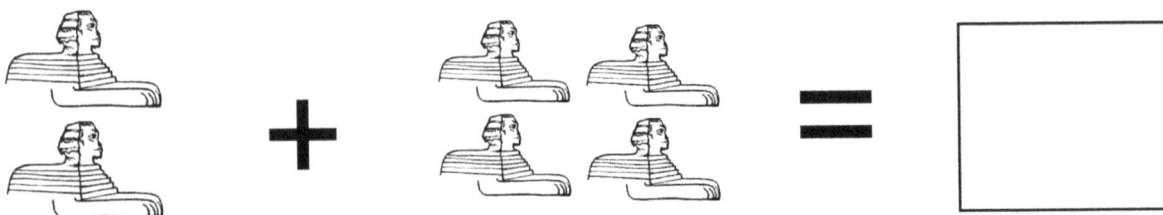

 + = ☐

 + = ☐

 + = ☐

 + = ☐

FRUIT COUNT

Circle the number that tells how many fruit there are! Count carefully!

2   4   5

8   6   7

7   2   1

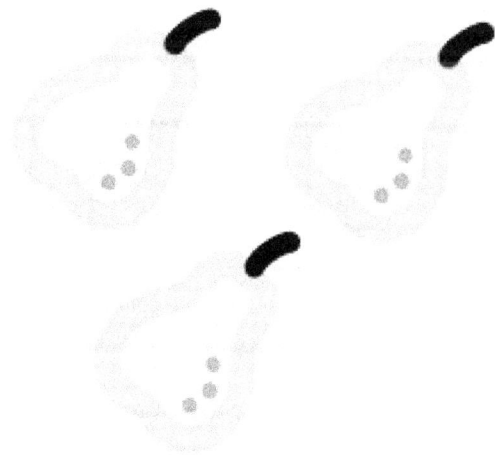

1   8   3

Count and Match

Directions: Count and glue correct number with the set.

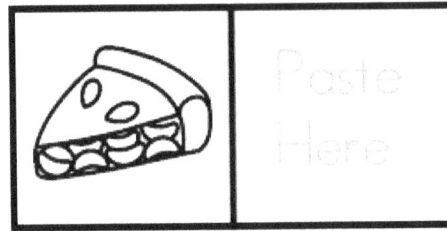

Set	Paste	Set	Paste
(2 acorns)	Paste Here	(4 leaves)	Paste Here
(4 pumpkins)	Paste Here	(1 pizza slice)	Paste Here
(2 scarecrow faces)	Paste Here	(3 leaves)	Paste Here
(4 apples)	Paste Here	(1 scarecrow)	Paste Here
(3 rakes)	Paste Here	(5 leaves)	Paste Here

1
4
2
5
3
1
3
2
4
5

Numbers 1-10

Directions: Cut and paste the numbers from 1-10 onto the train.

3	8	5	10	2
6	1	9	4	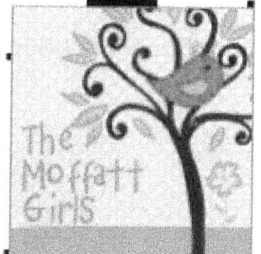

3   3   3   3

3   3

3   2   2

3

2   2

3   2

2   2   2   2

2

3

2

2

3   2

2   3   3

2

3   3   3

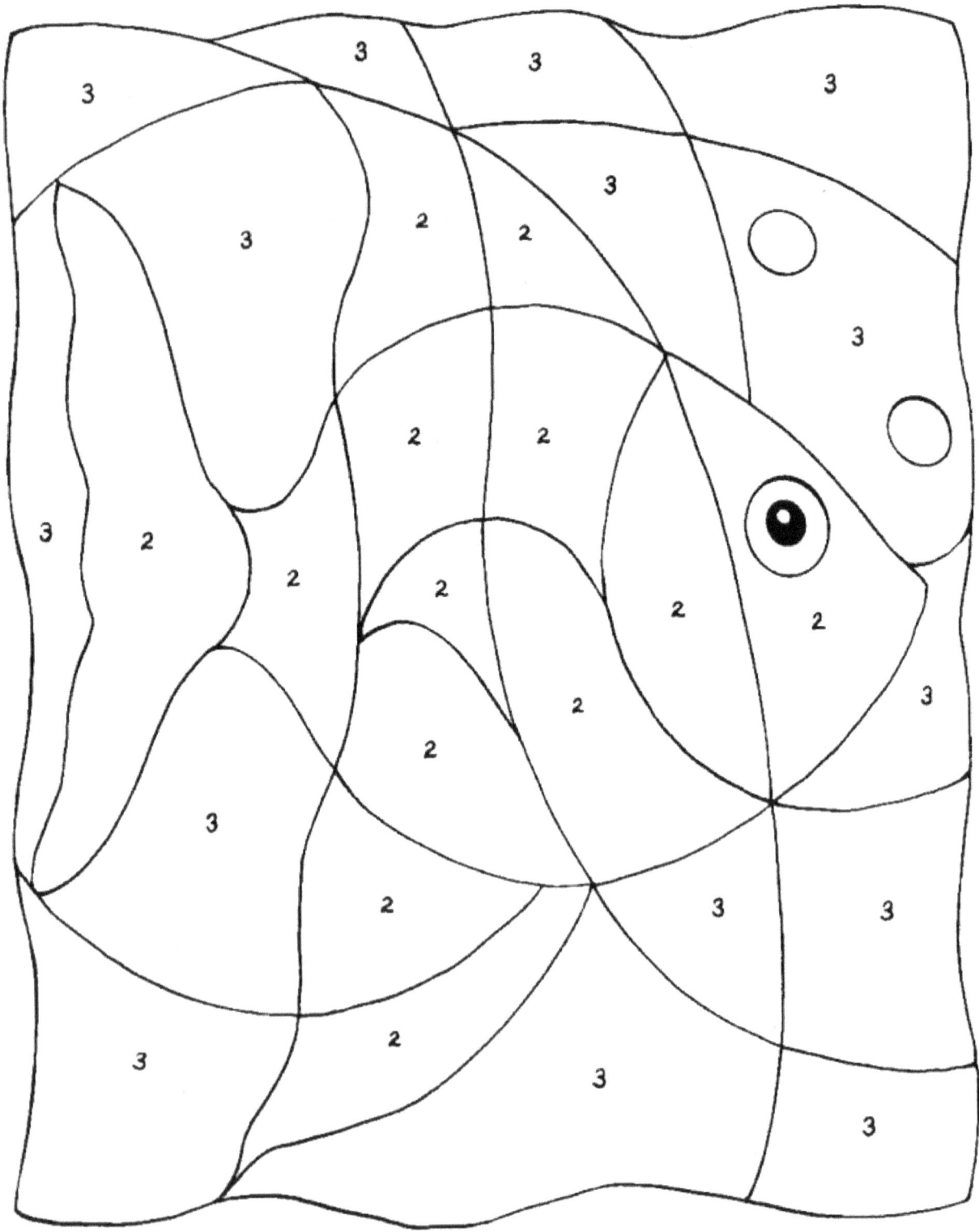

Color the 2's yellow and the 3's blue

94

Before and After Numbers

Directions: Write the numbers that come before and after the numbers on the watering cans.

☐ 🪣 13 ☐   ☐ 🪣 10 ☐

☐ 🪣 16 ☐   ☐ 🪣 14 ☐

☐ 🪣 11 ☐   ☐ 🪣 19 ☐

☐ 🪣 15 ☐   ☐ 🪣 12 ☐

☐ 🪣 17 ☐   ☐ 🪣 20 ☐

☐ 🪣 9 ☐   ☐ 🪣 18 ☐

Write each missing number.

1 ◯ 3 ◯ 5 ◯ ◯ 8

9 ◯ 11 ◯ 13 ◯ ◯ 16

17 ◯ 19 ◯ 21 ◯ ◯ 24

25 ◯ 27 ◯ 29 ◯ ◯ 32

33 ◯ 35 ◯ 37 ◯ ◯ 40

41 ◯ 43 ◯ 45 ◯ ◯ 48

49 50

NUMBERS 1-10

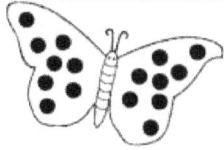	1
	2
	3
	4
	5
	6
	7
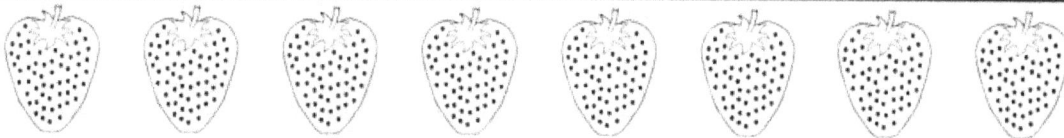	8
	9
	10

Name _____

Farmer Bob has to take some chicks to his friend's house. He needs your help coloring only the chicks with number 3 on them and counting how many there are.

Answer: _____

Name_____

Use the code below to color the picture.

1¢	50¢
25¢	25¢
50¢	1¢
1¢	5¢
1¢	25¢
50¢	5¢
10¢	10¢

penny- yellow   nickel- purple   dime- dark green   quarter- red
two dimes- brown   two quarters- blue   two pennies- light green

ORNAMENT ☆ NOTES

Color the A pink
Color the B green.
Color the C orange
Color the D yellow

Color the E purple.
Color the F's blue.
Color the G's red.
Color the Christmas tree.

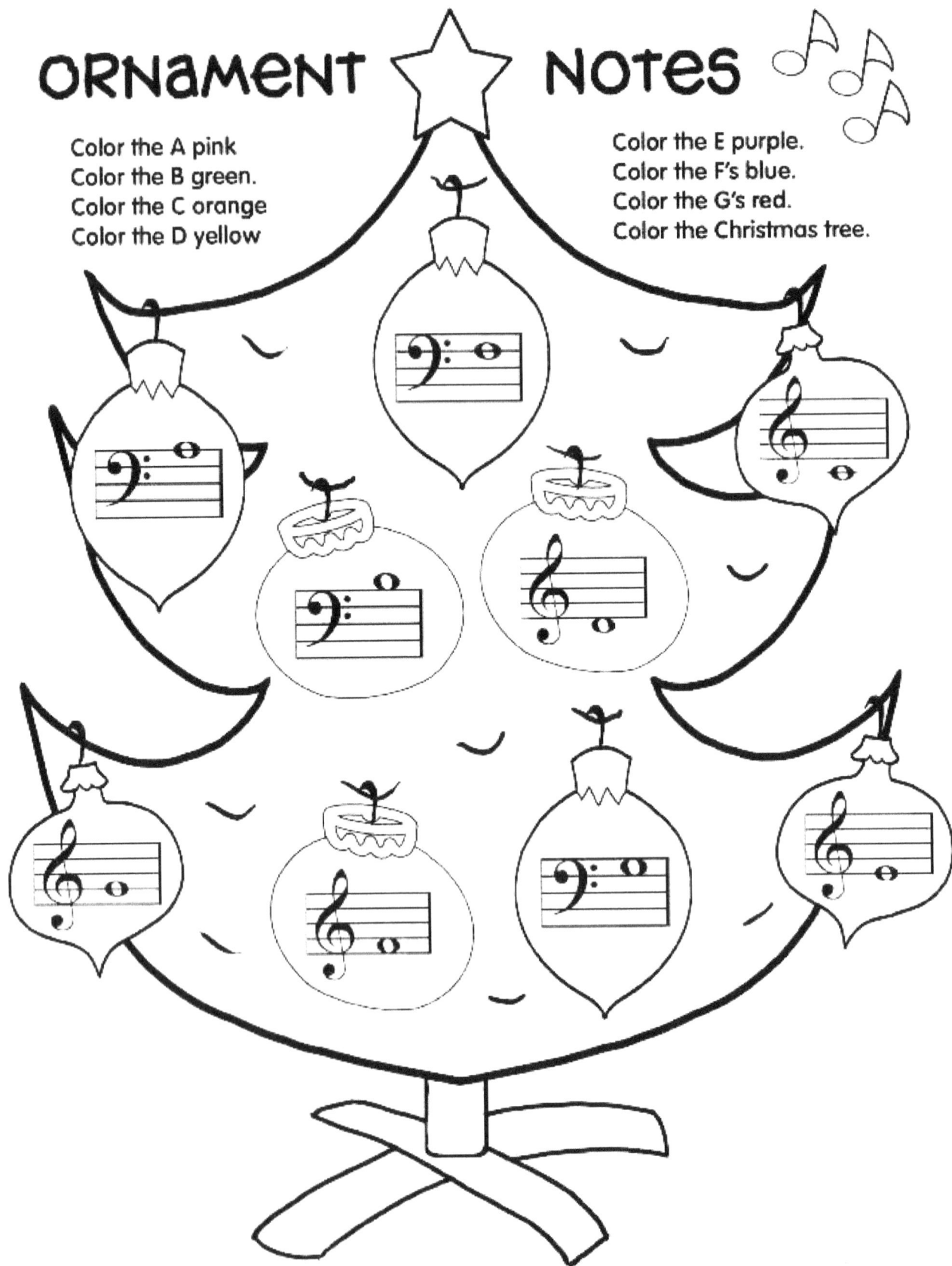

YOU'RE SO SMART!

COLOR ME

www.ingramcontent.com/pod-product-compliance
Lightning Source LLC
Chambersburg PA
CBHW081257040426
42452CB00014B/2542